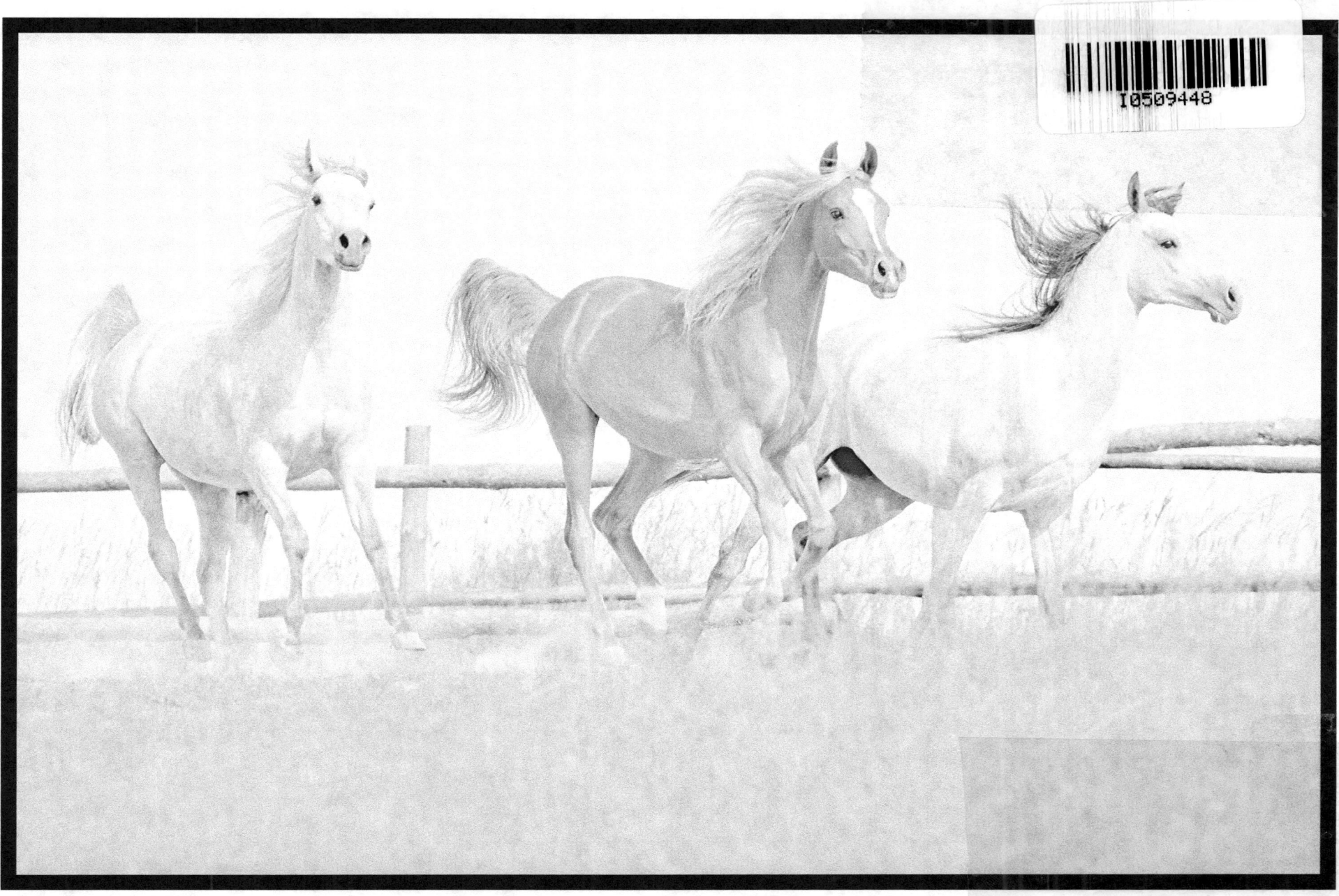

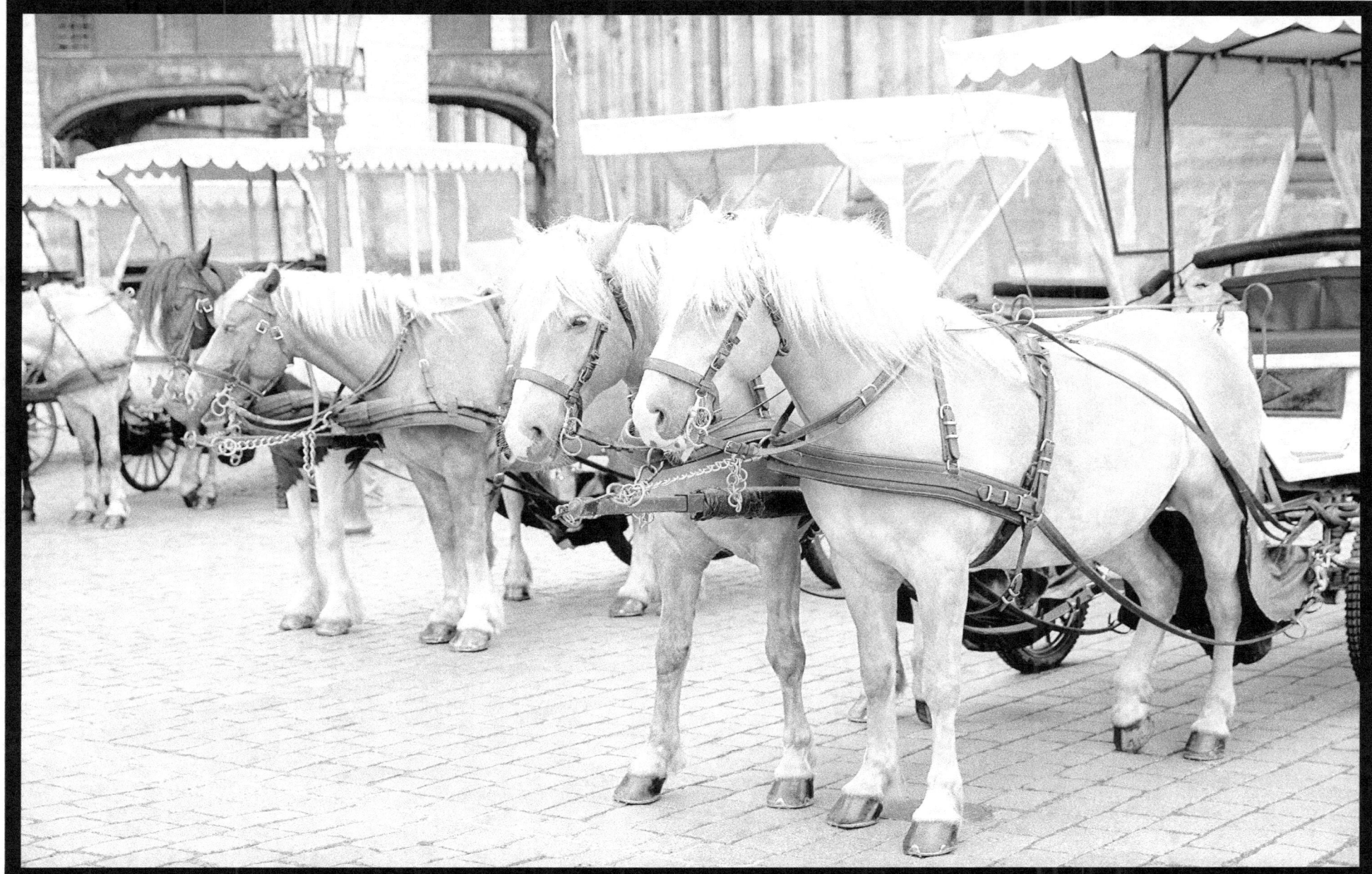

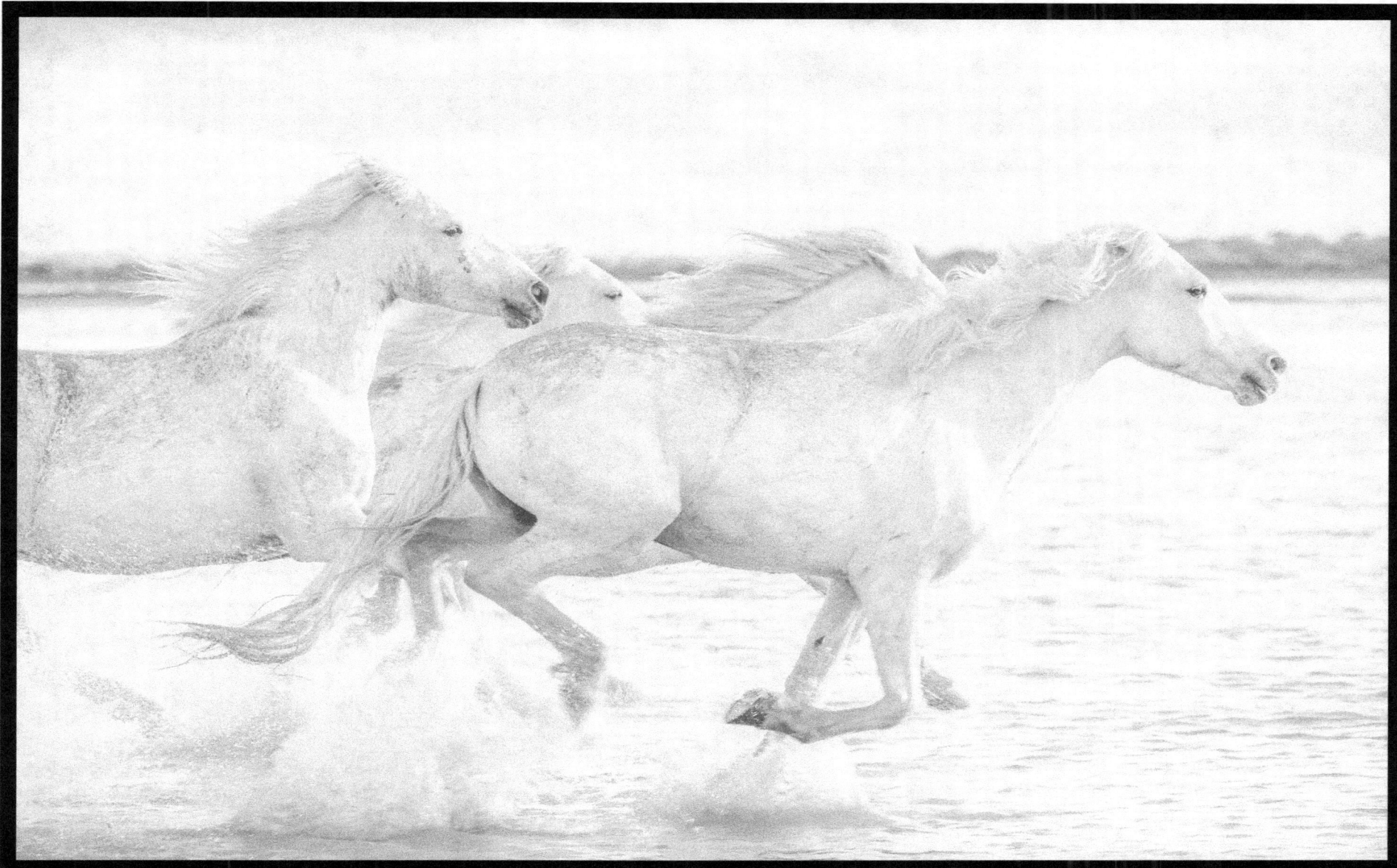

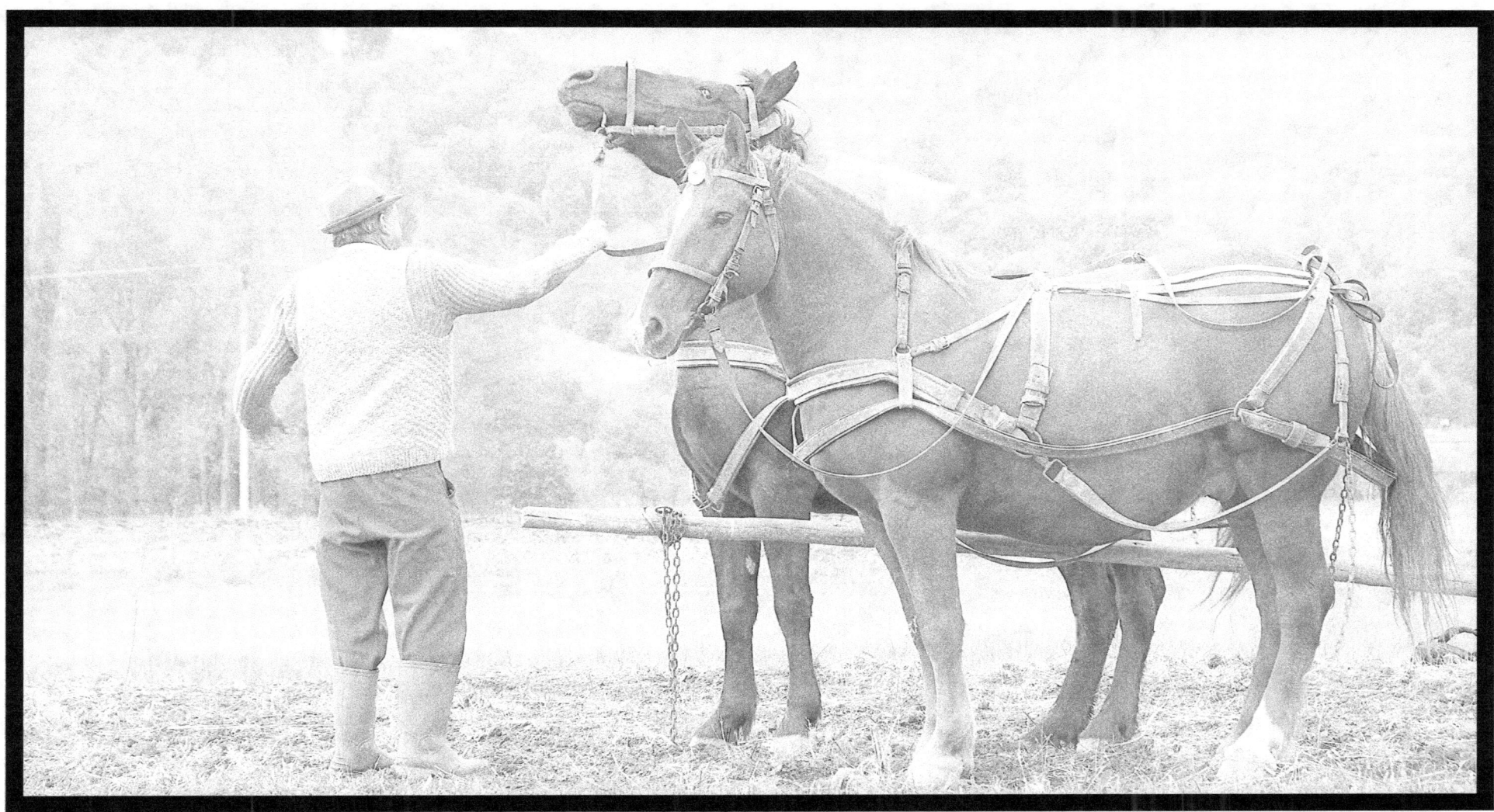

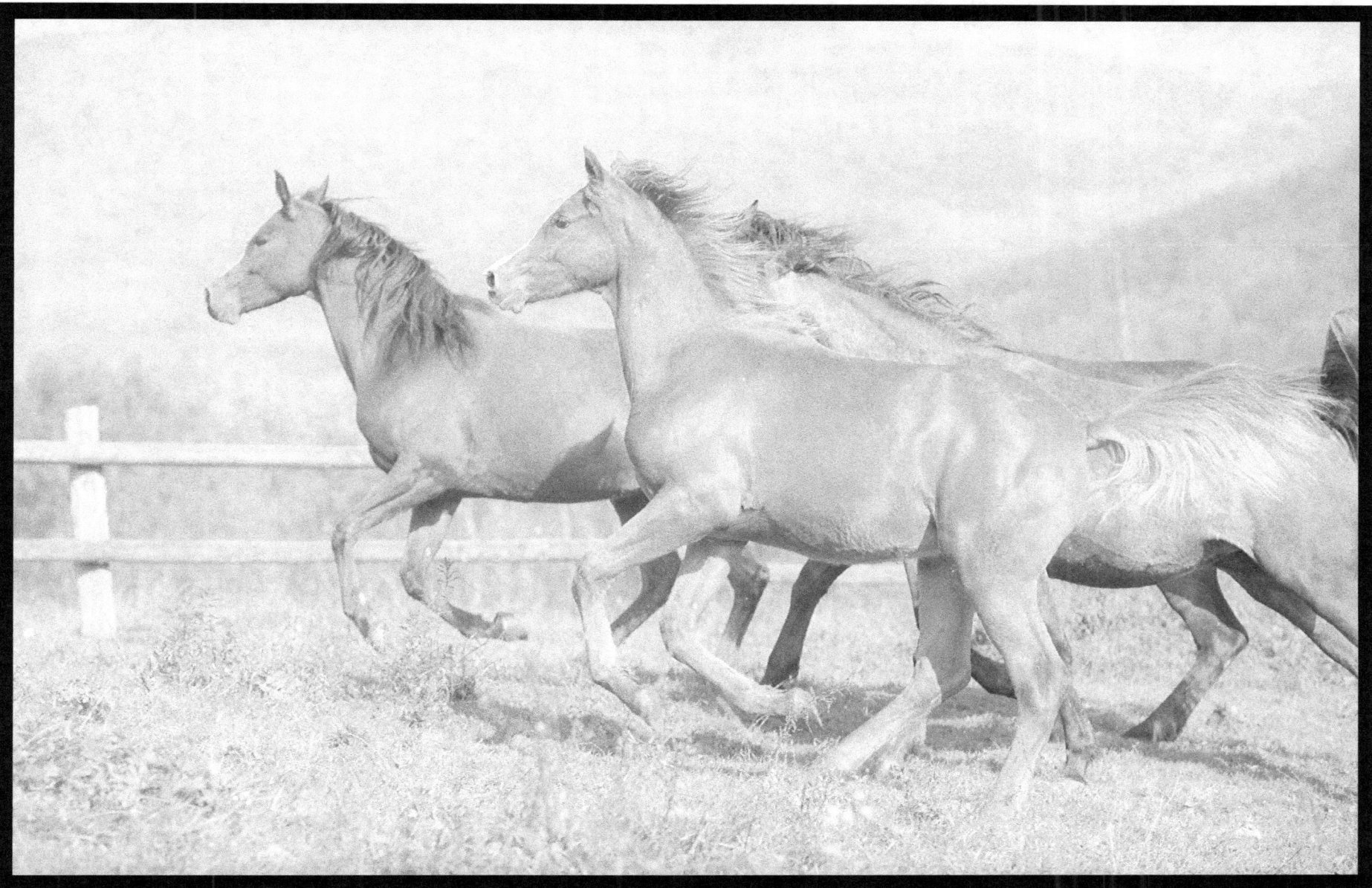

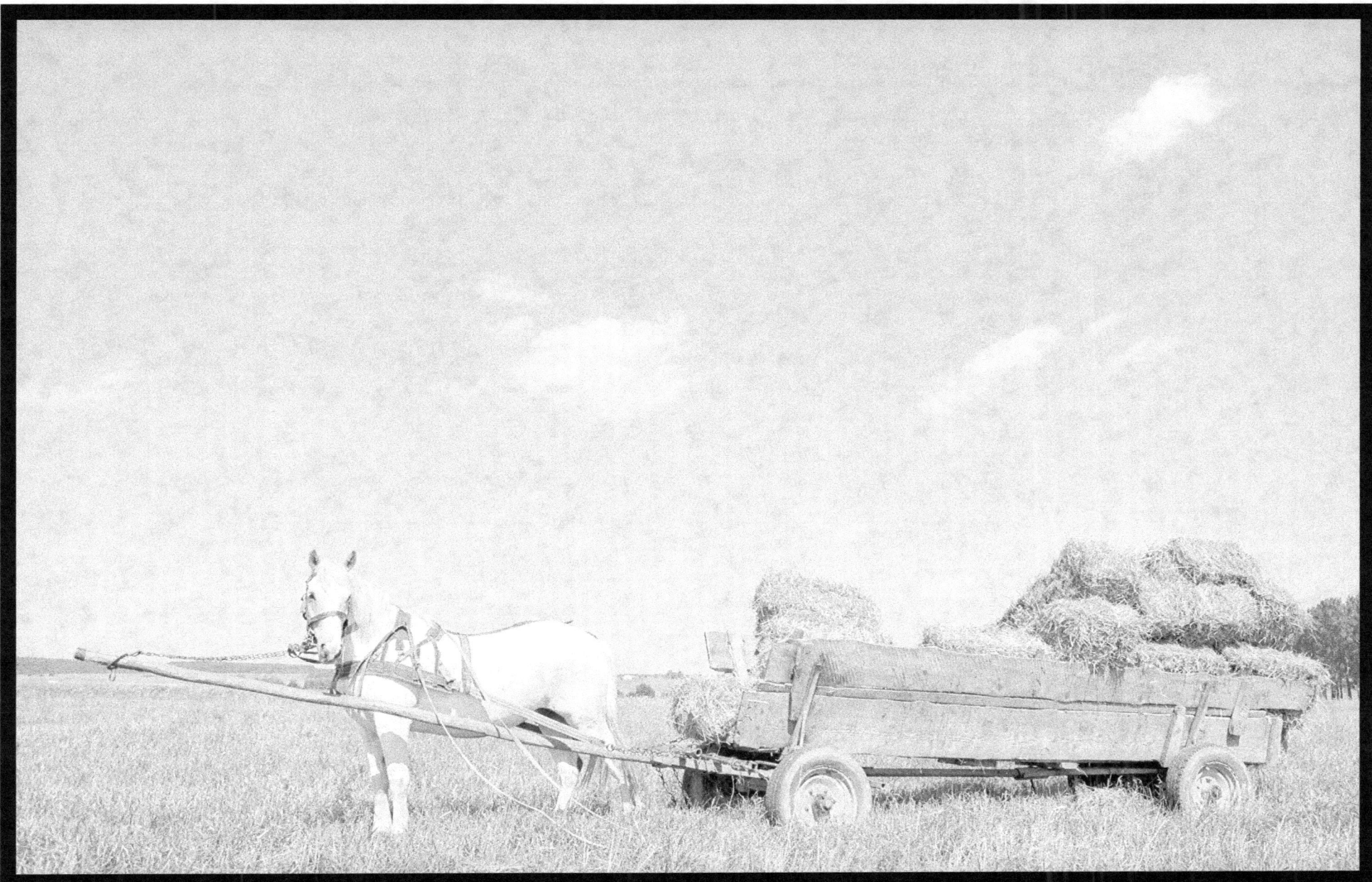

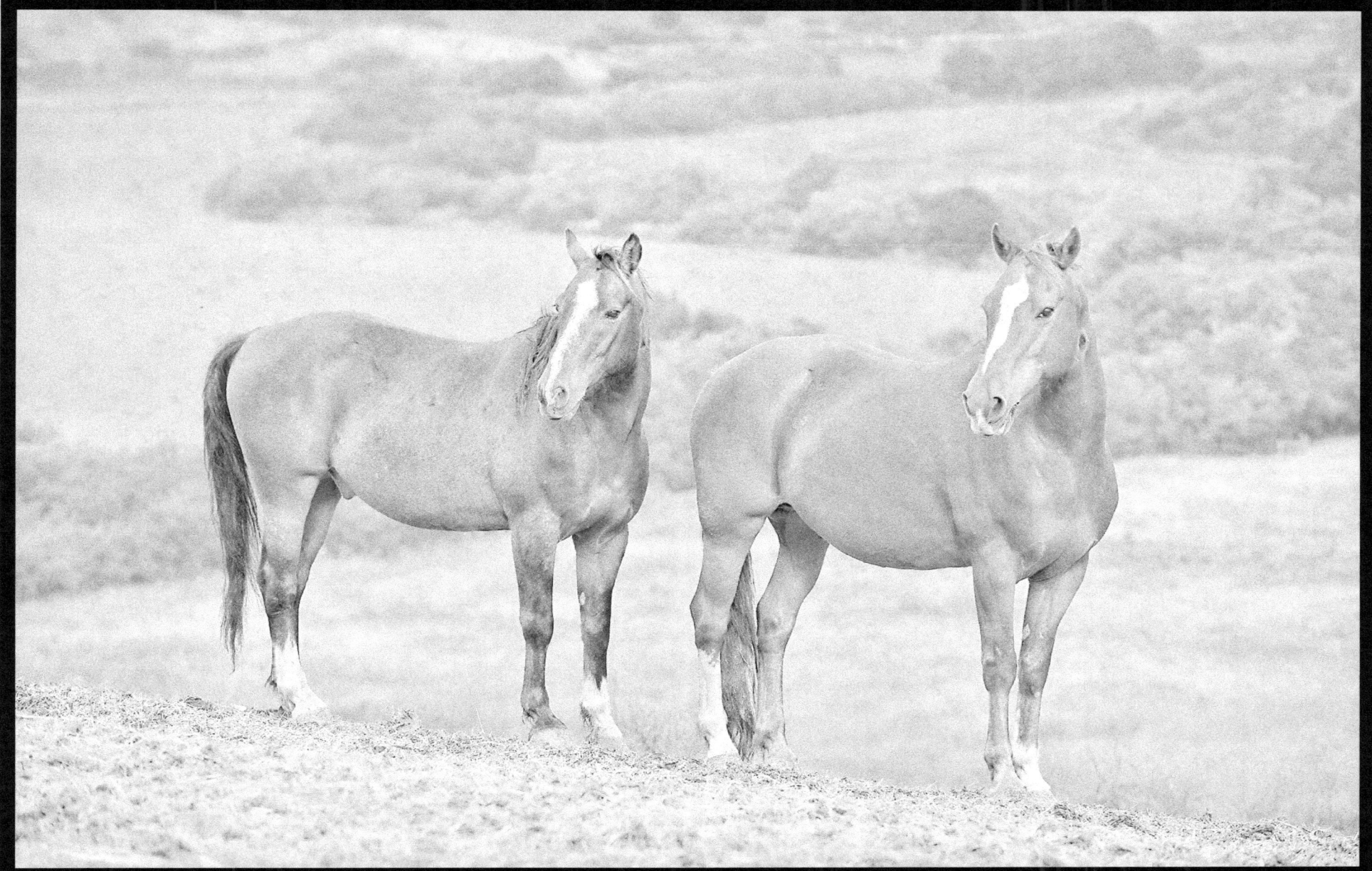

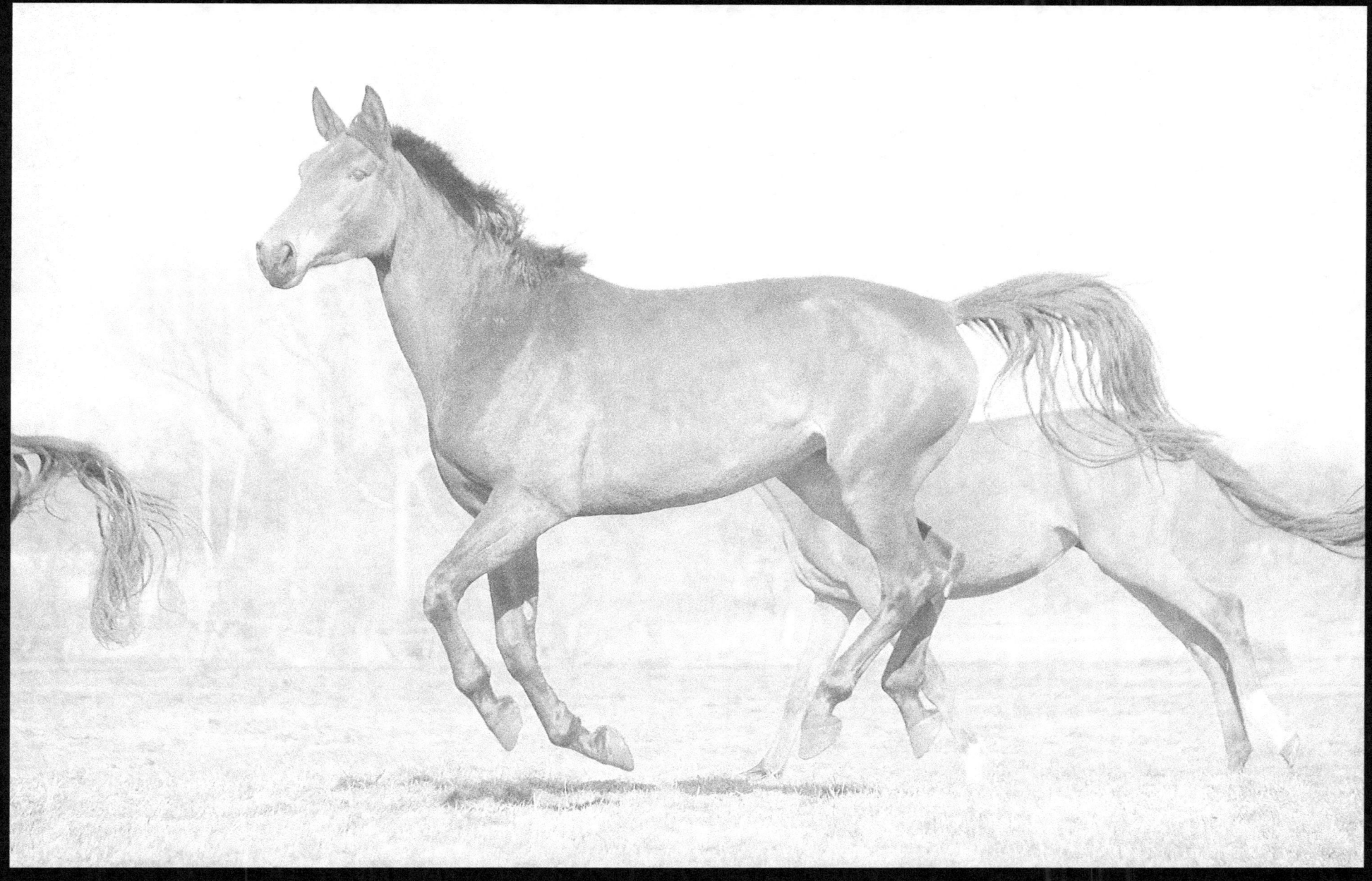

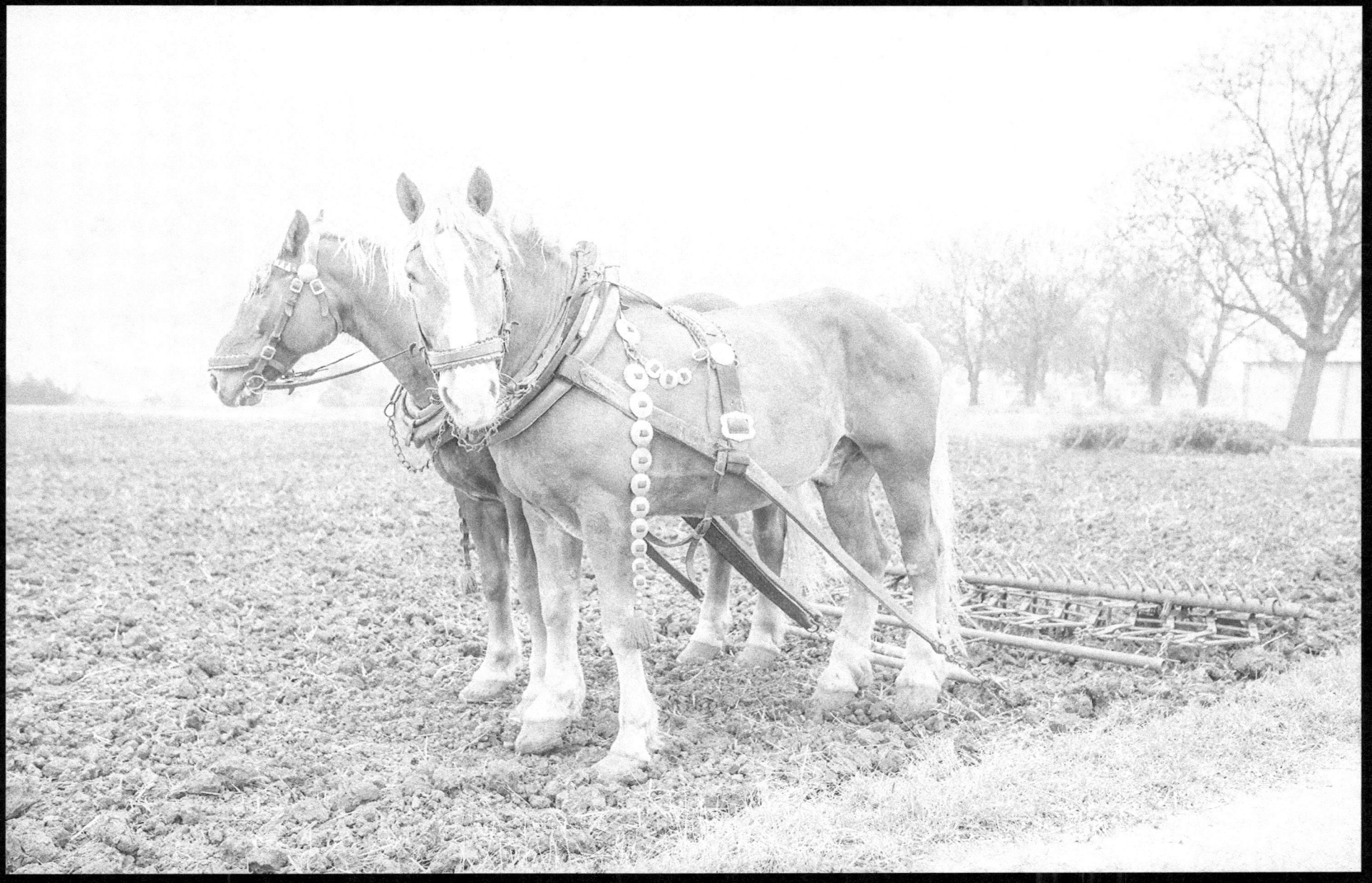

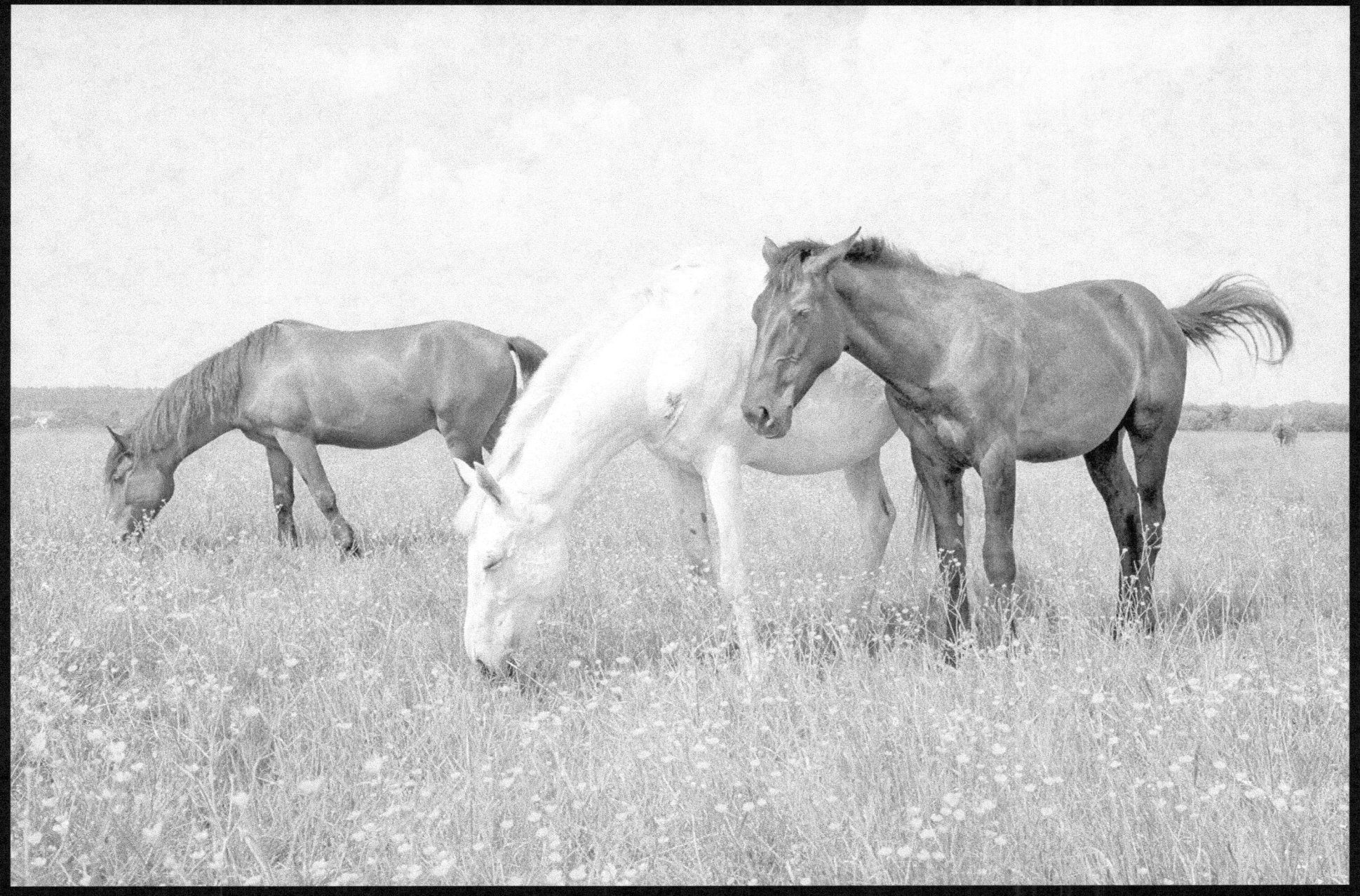

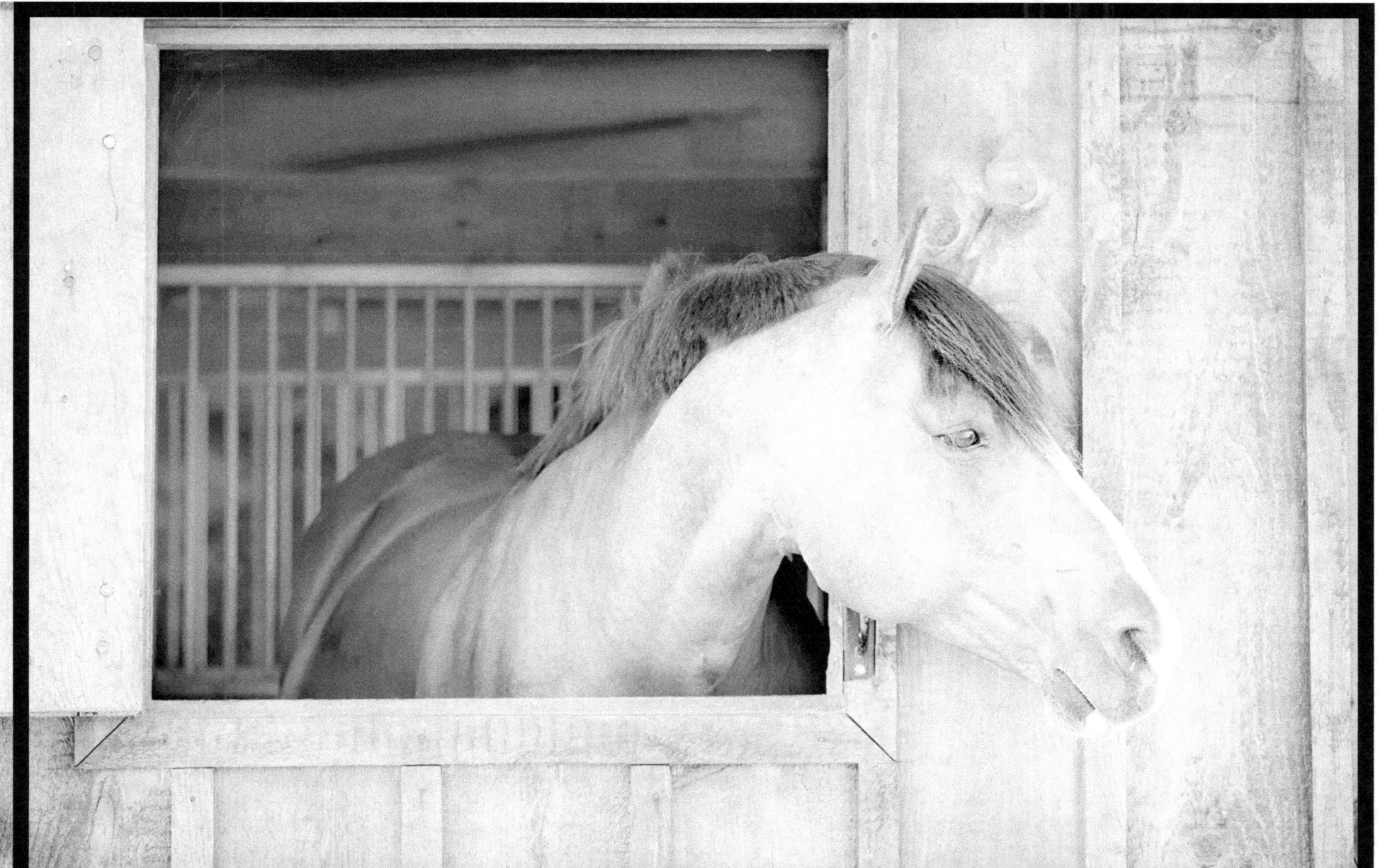

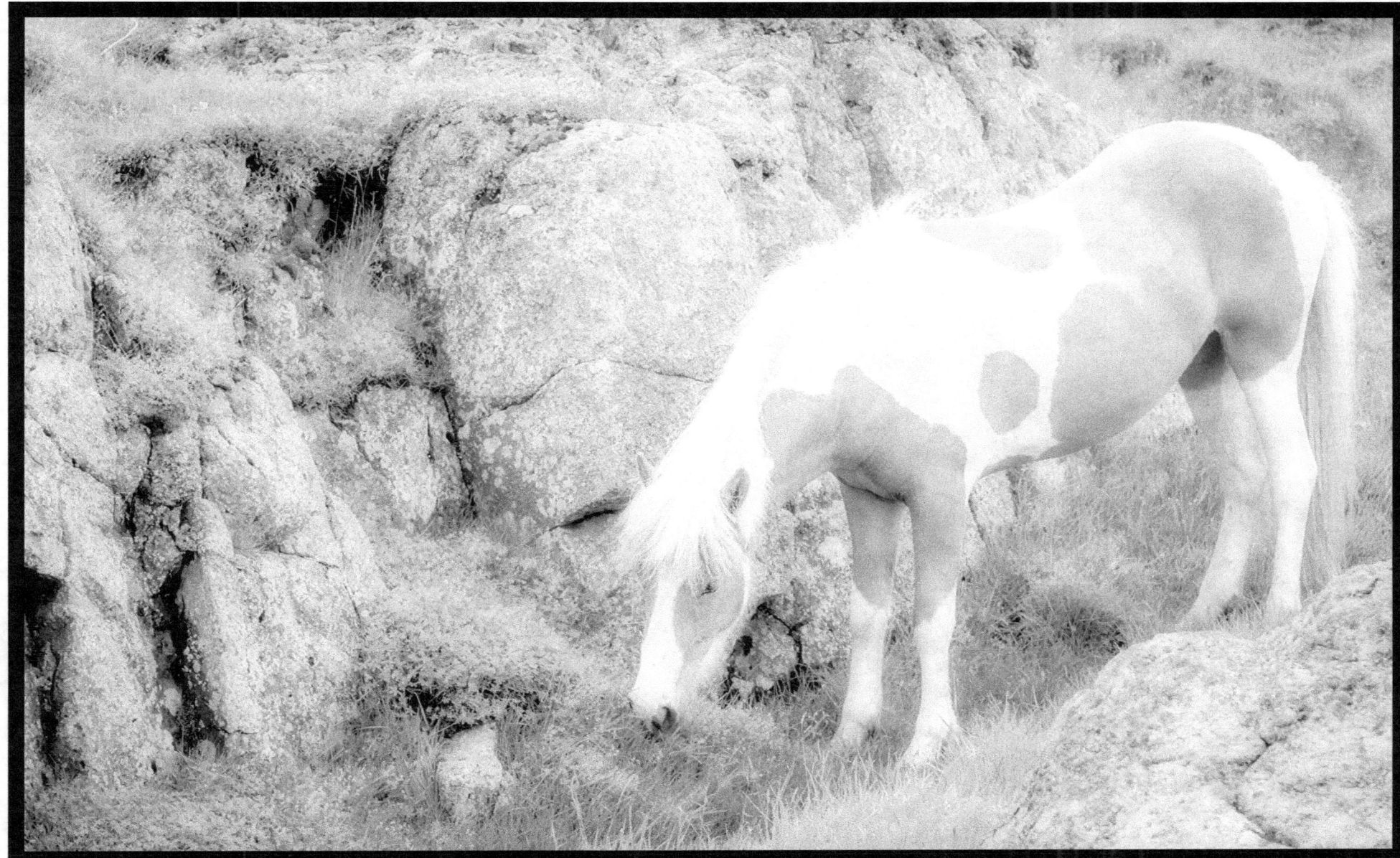

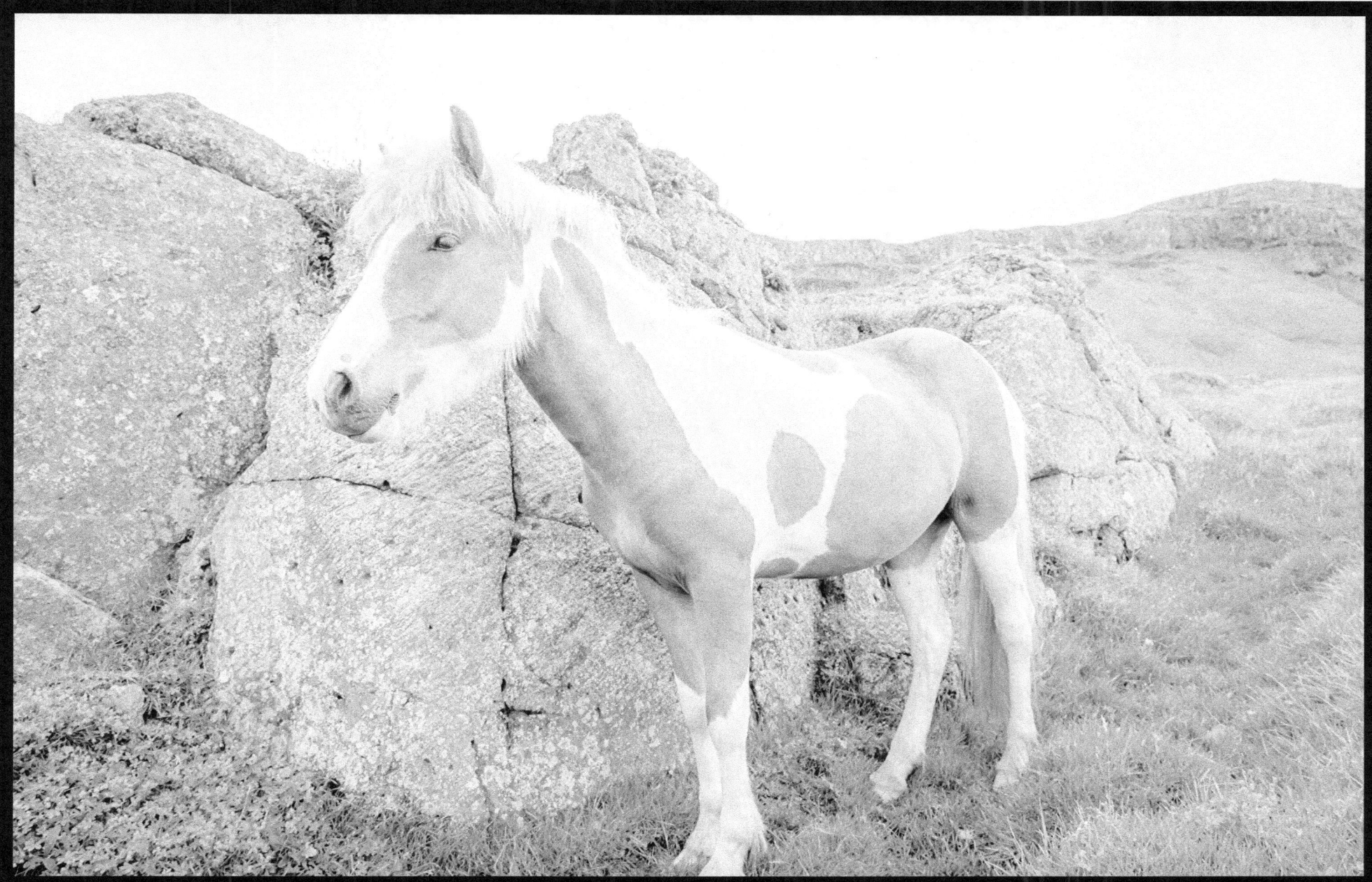

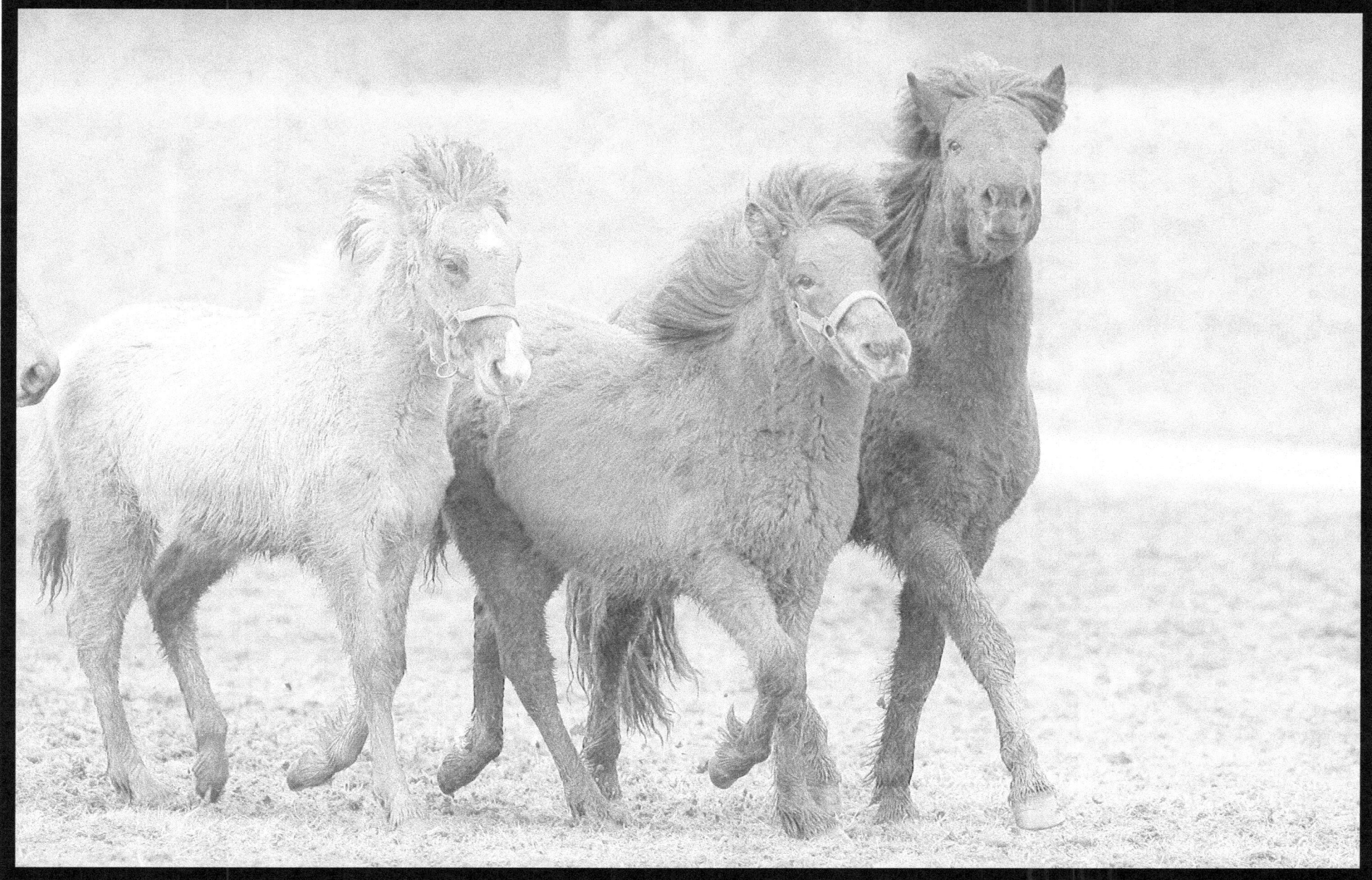

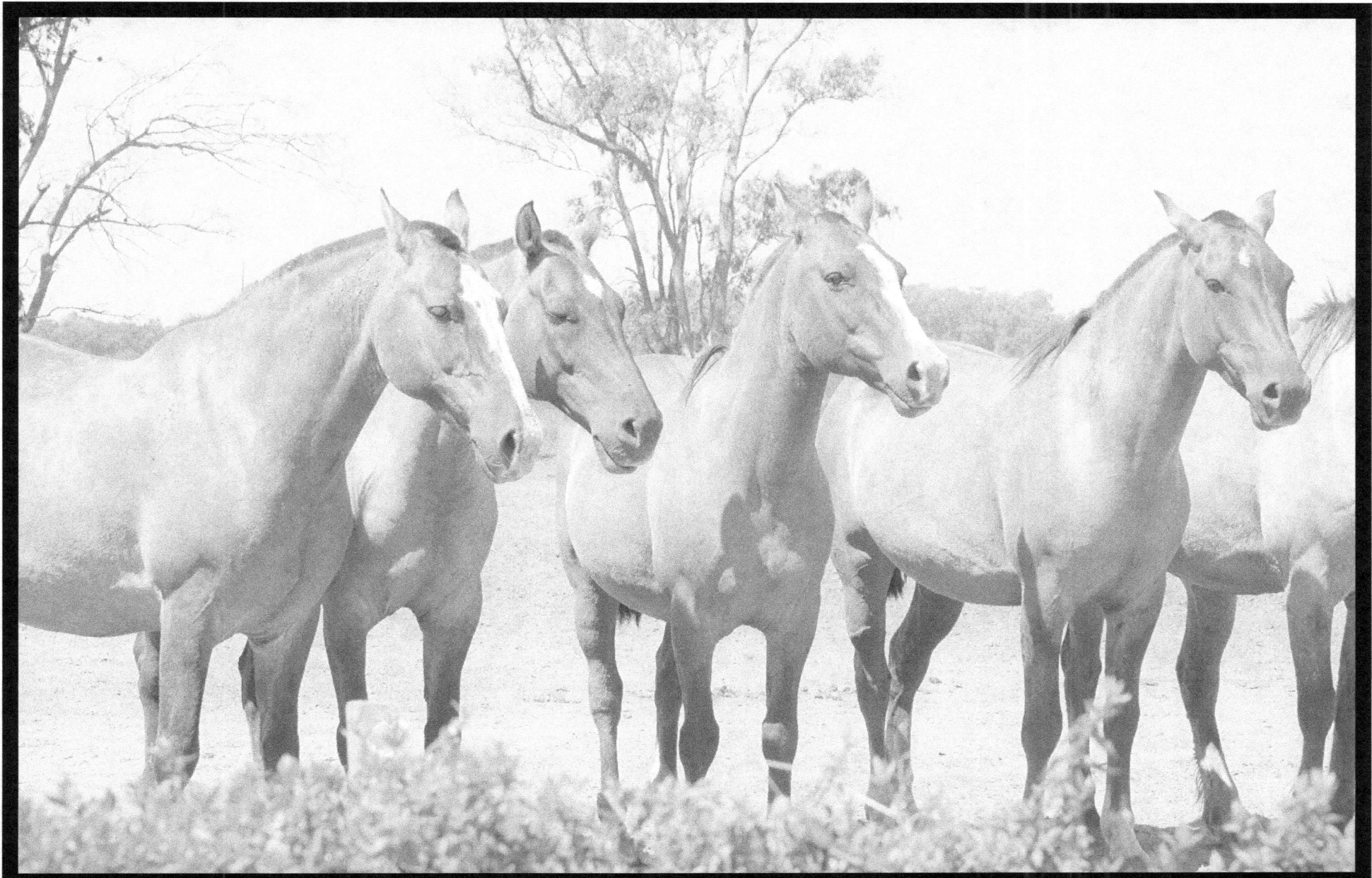

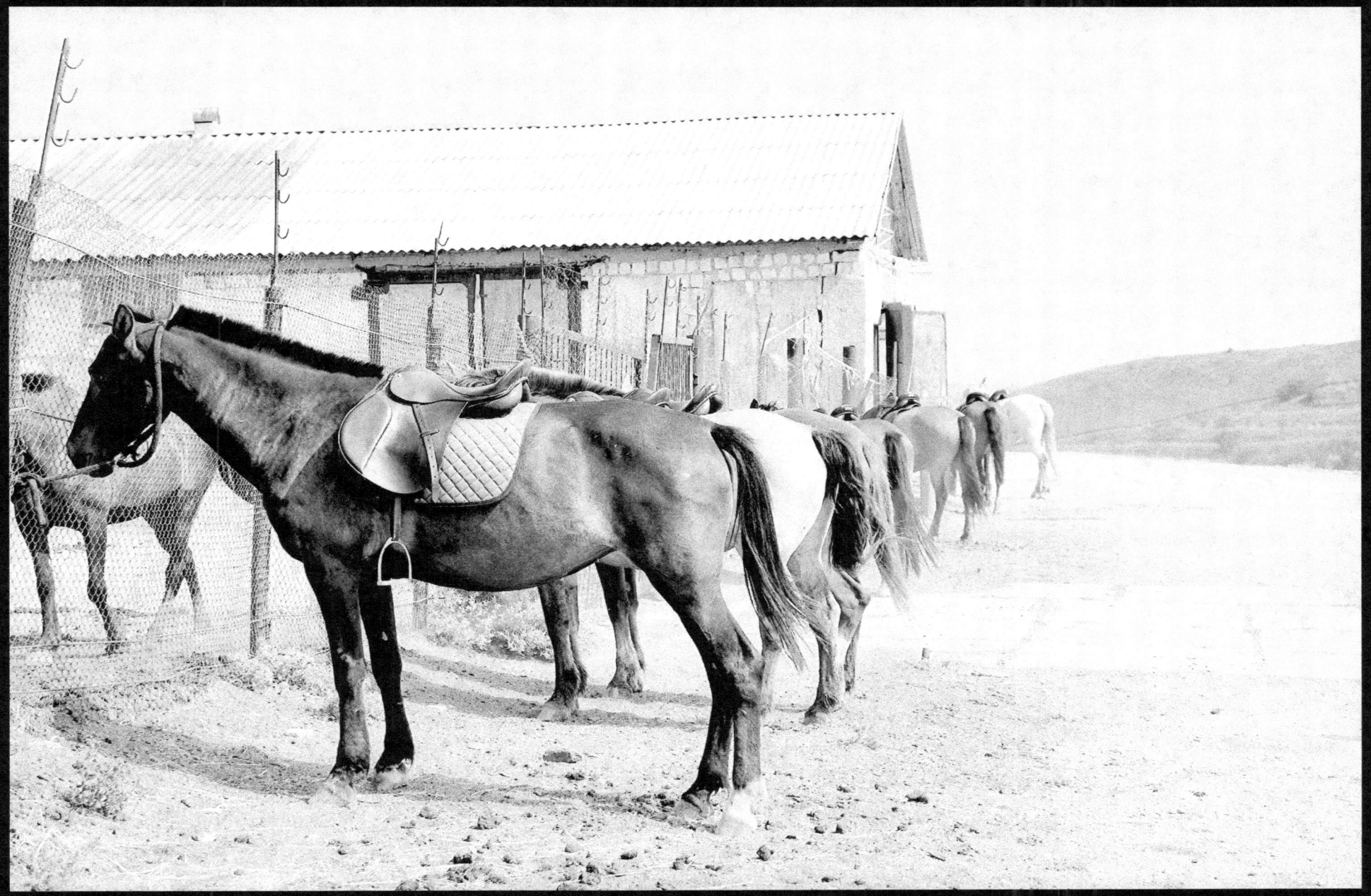

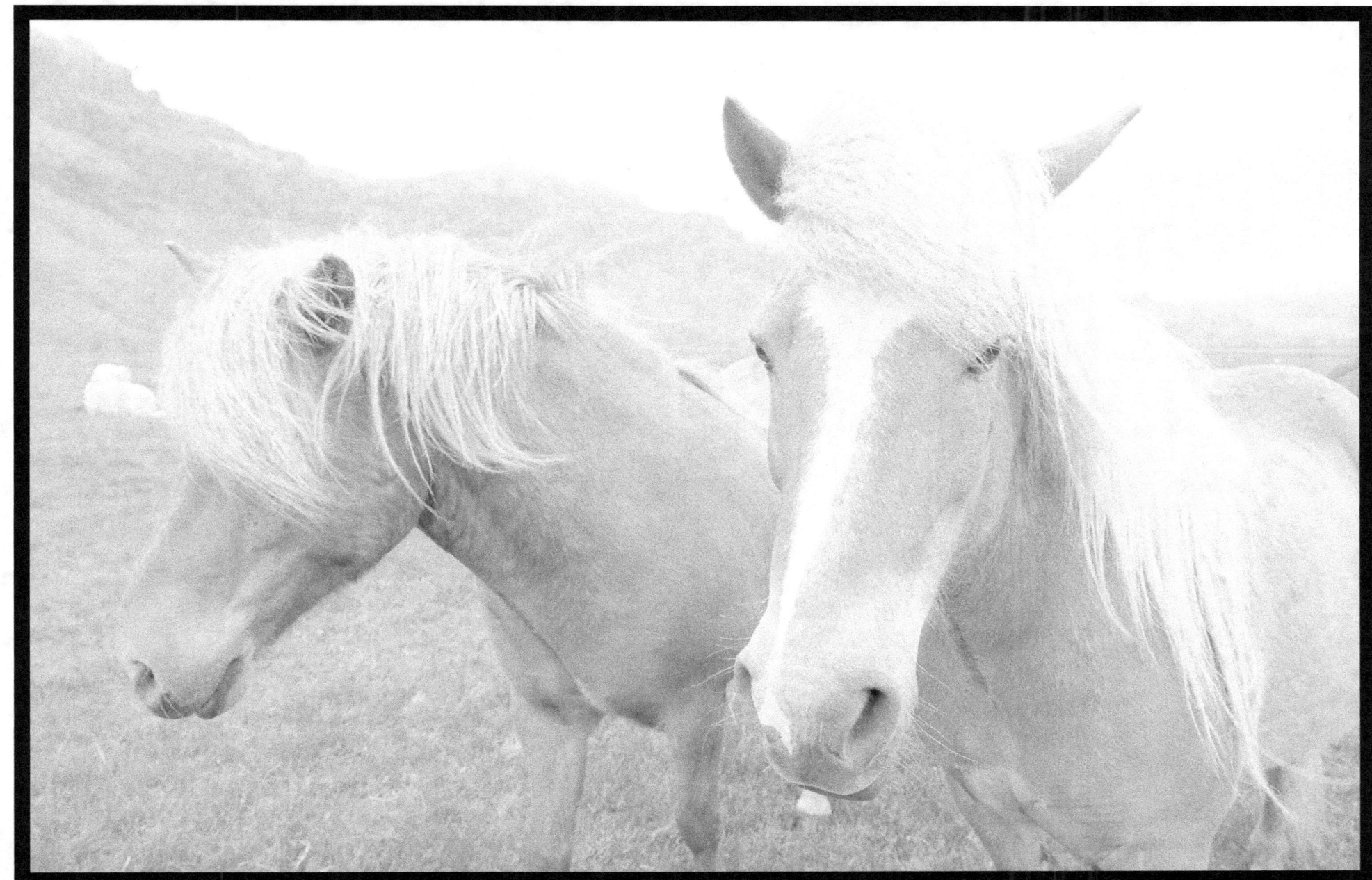

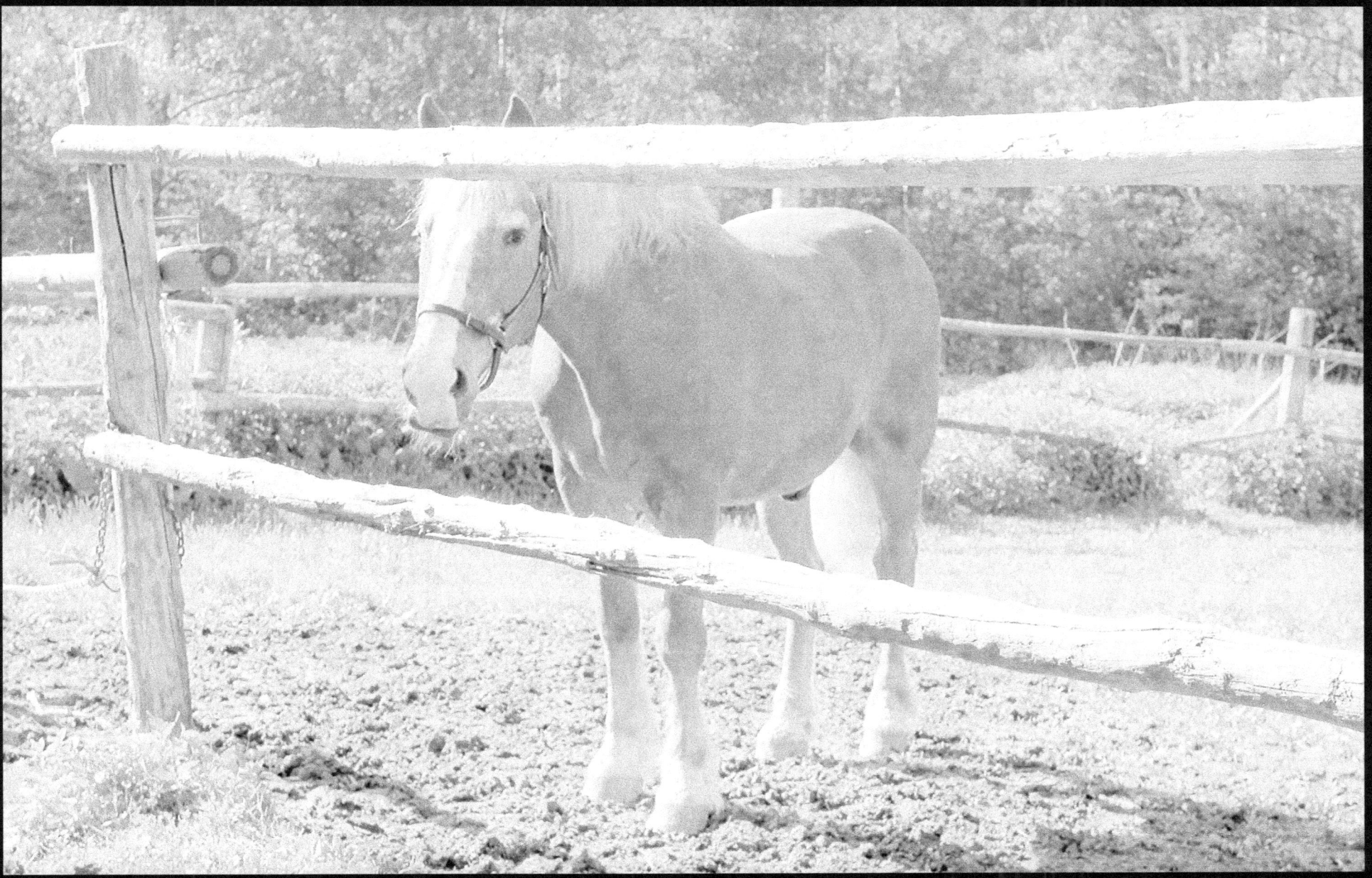

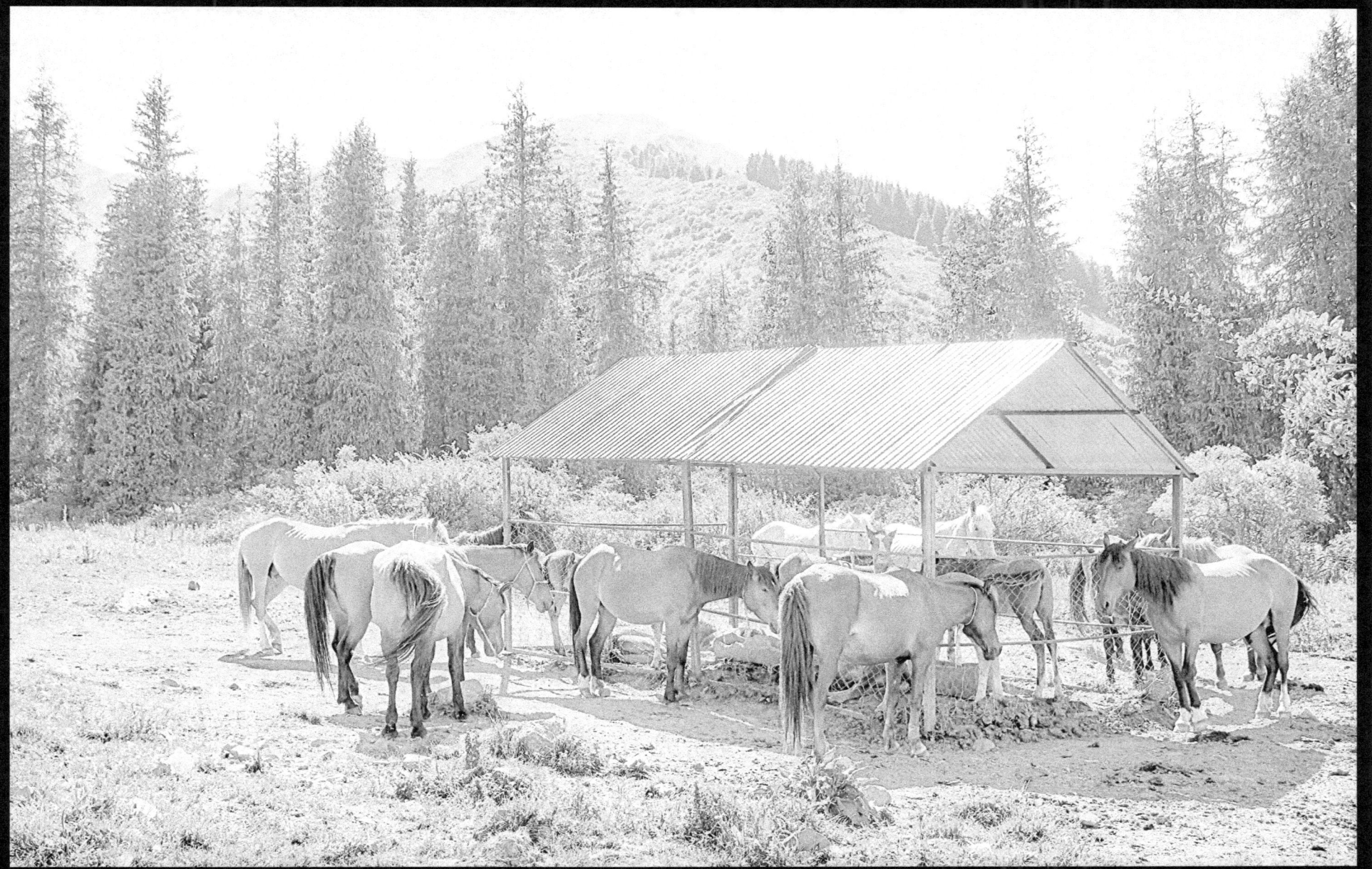

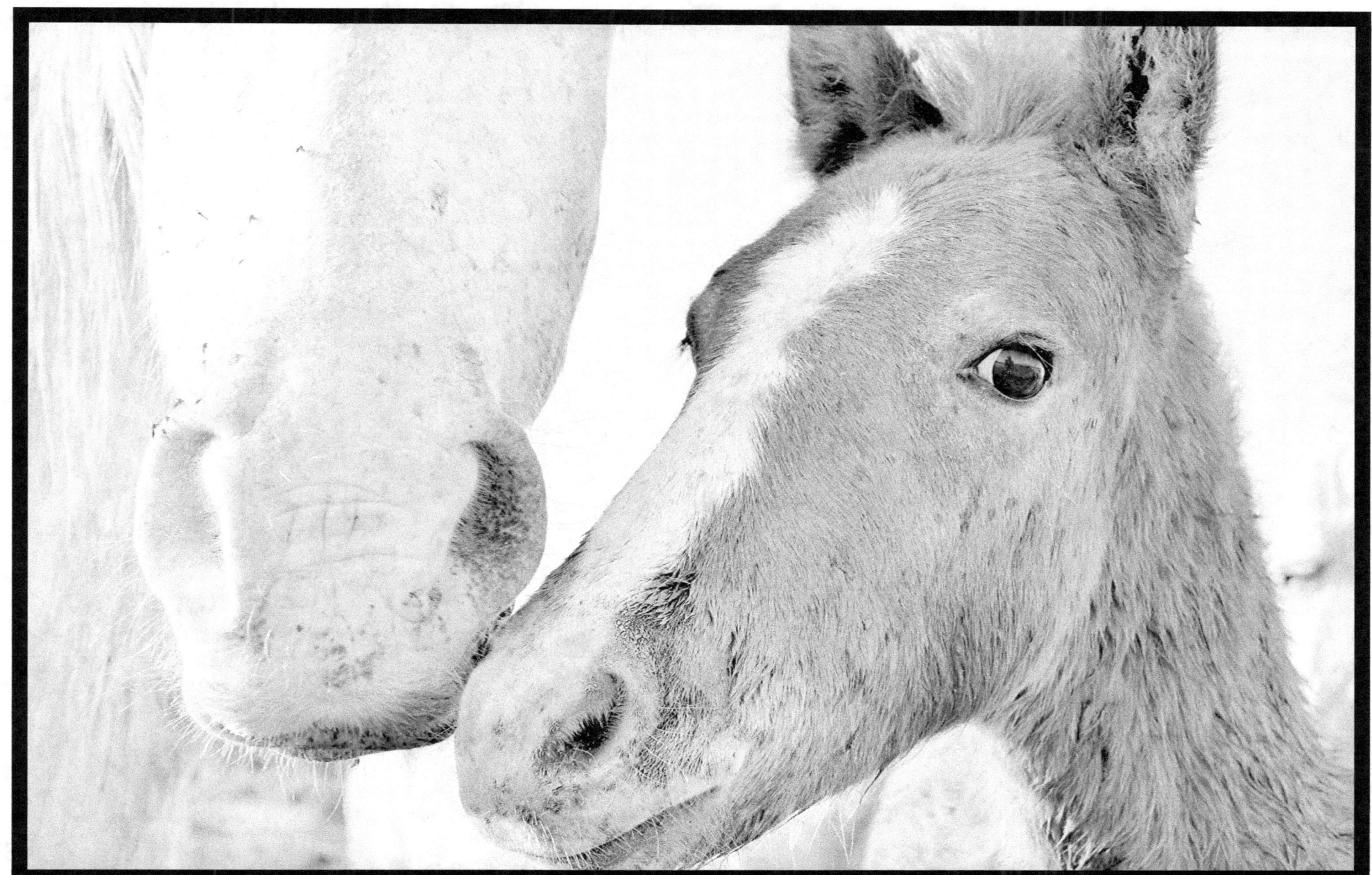

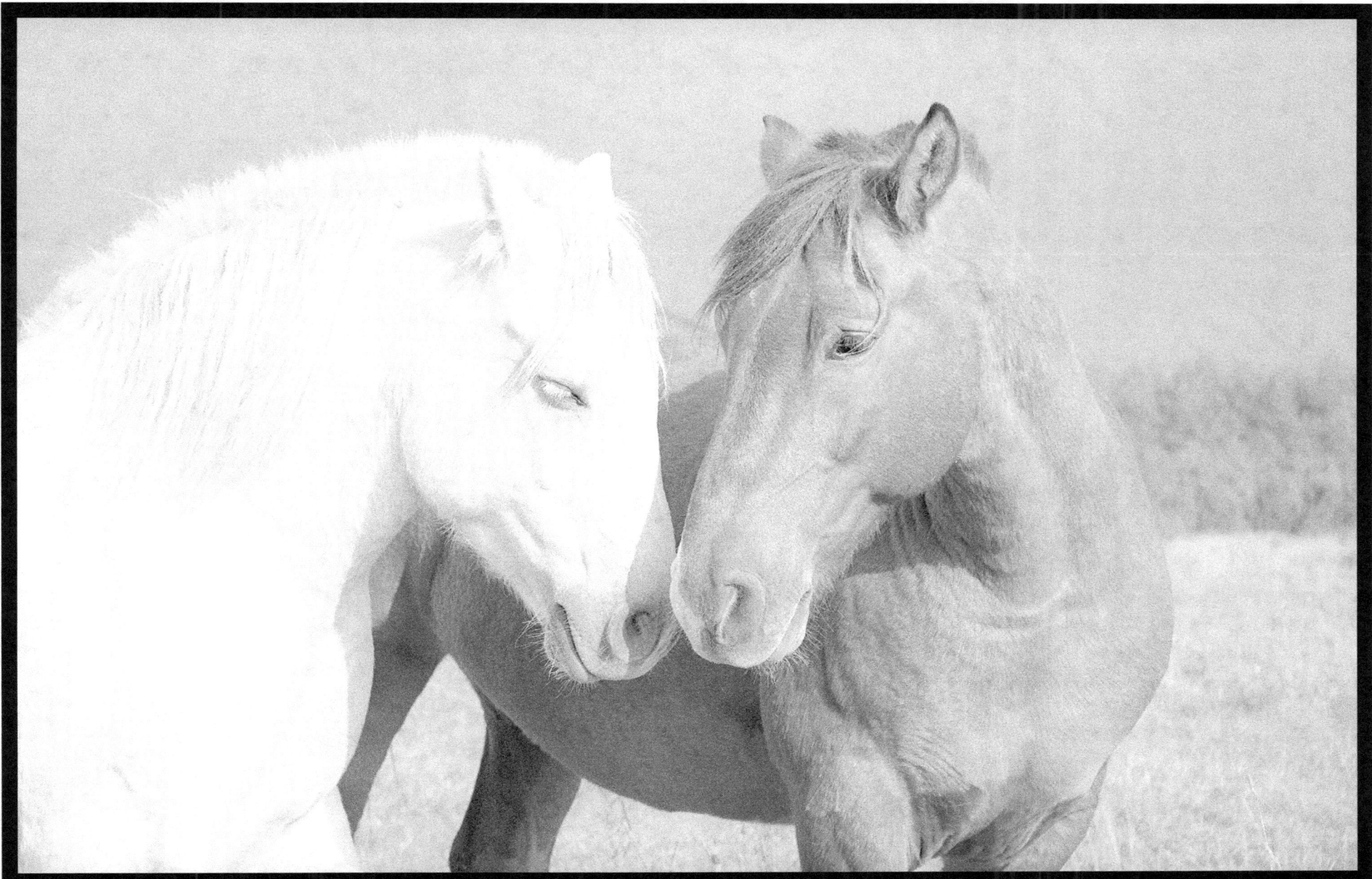

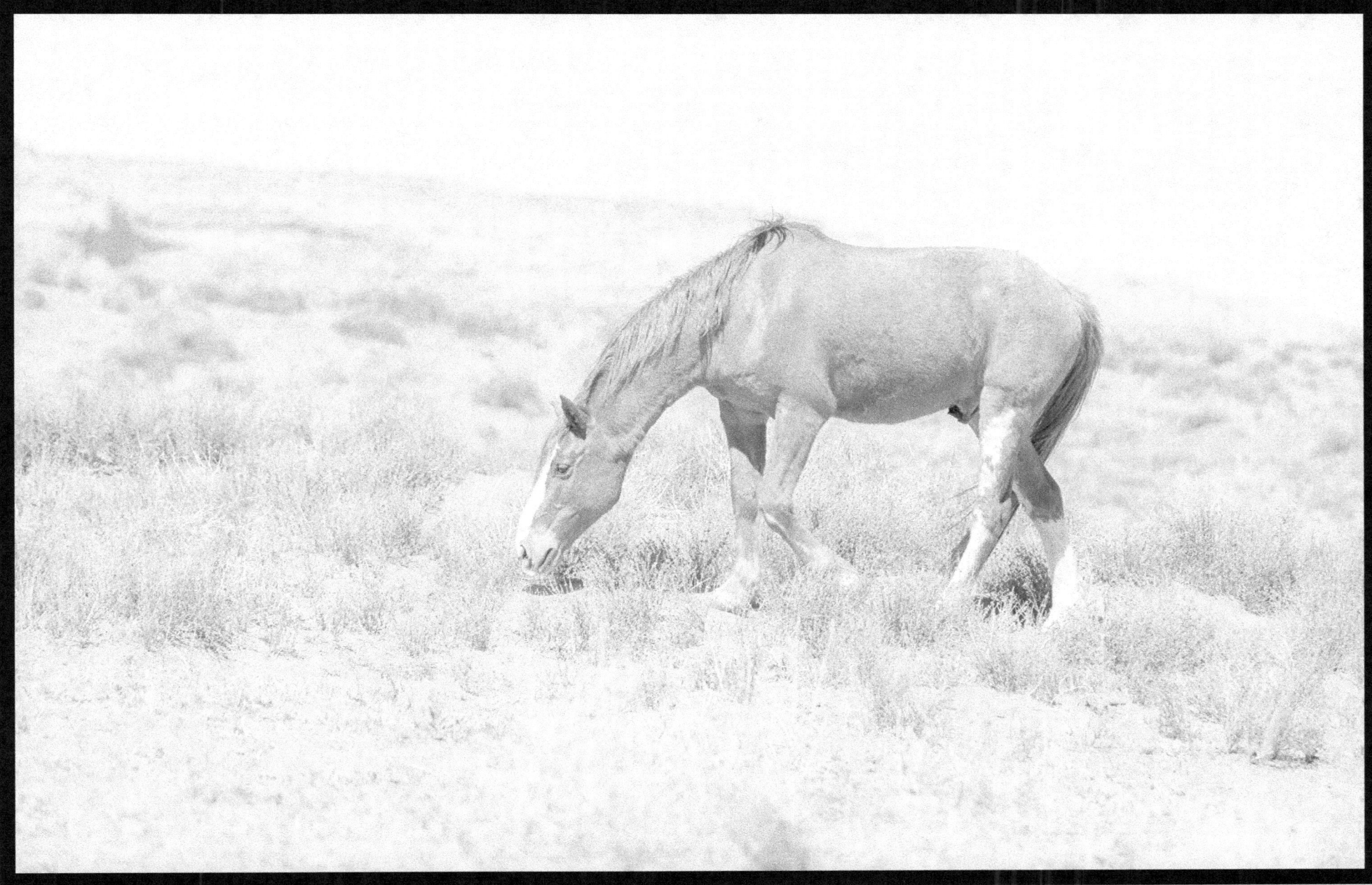

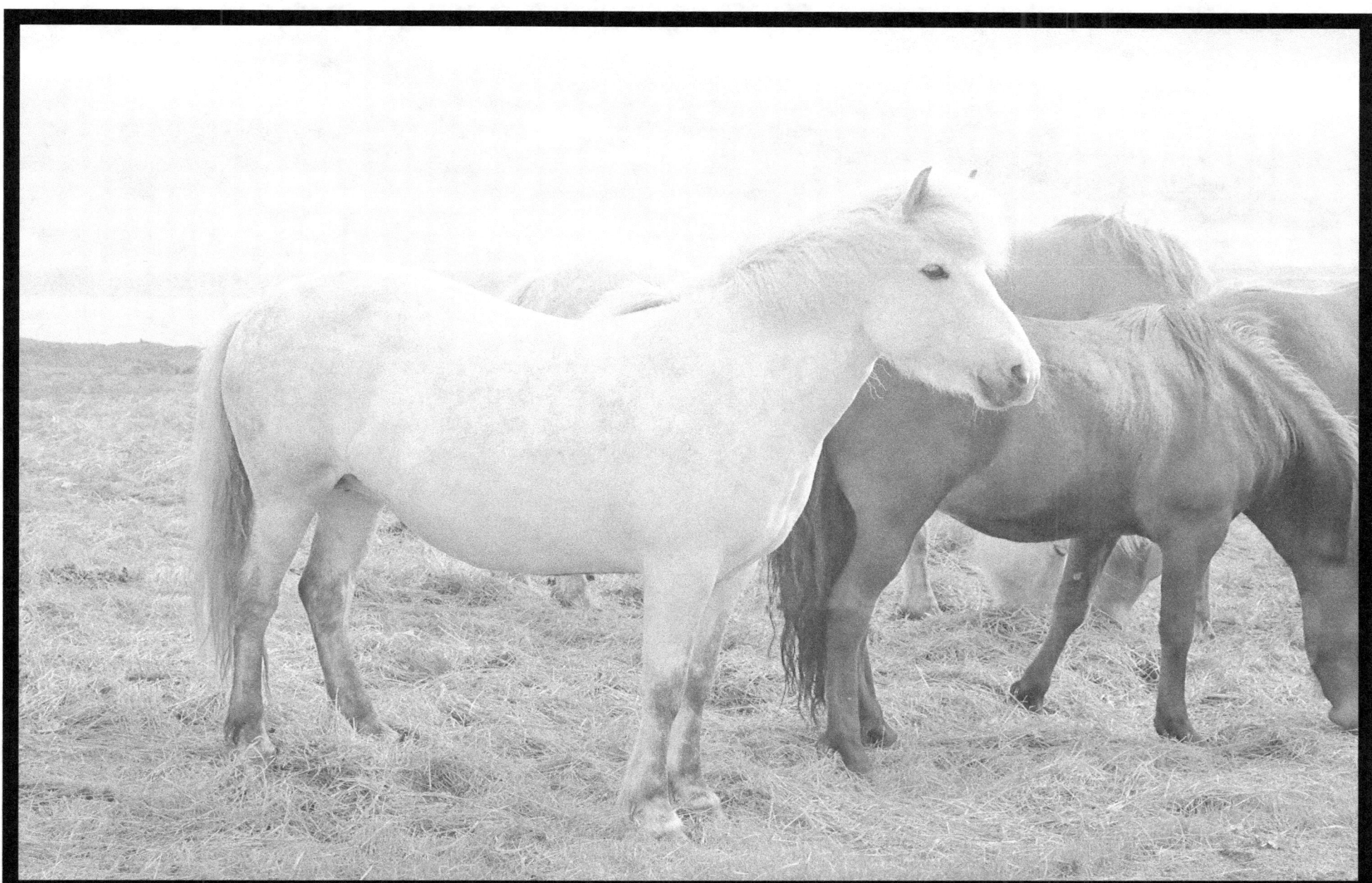

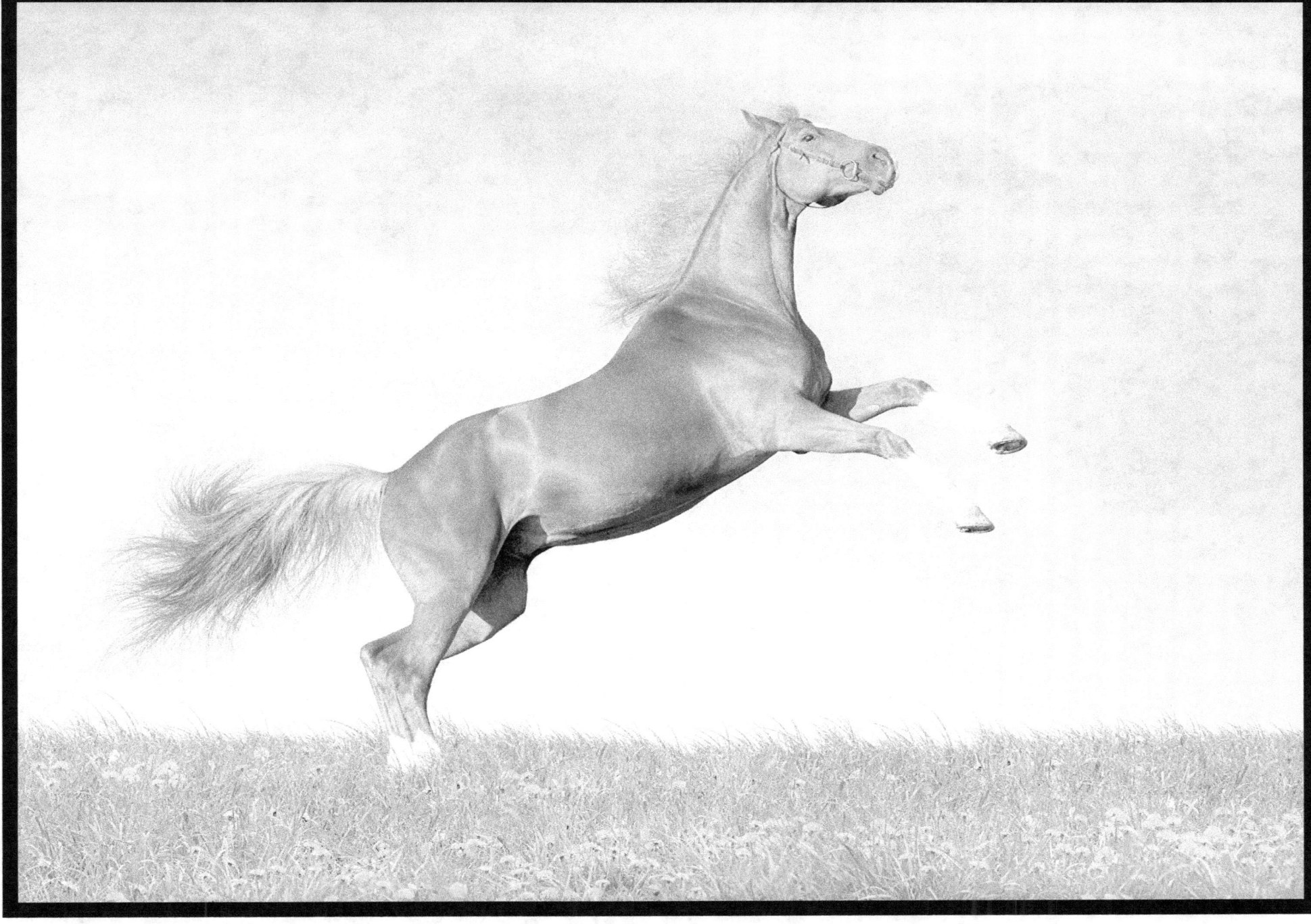

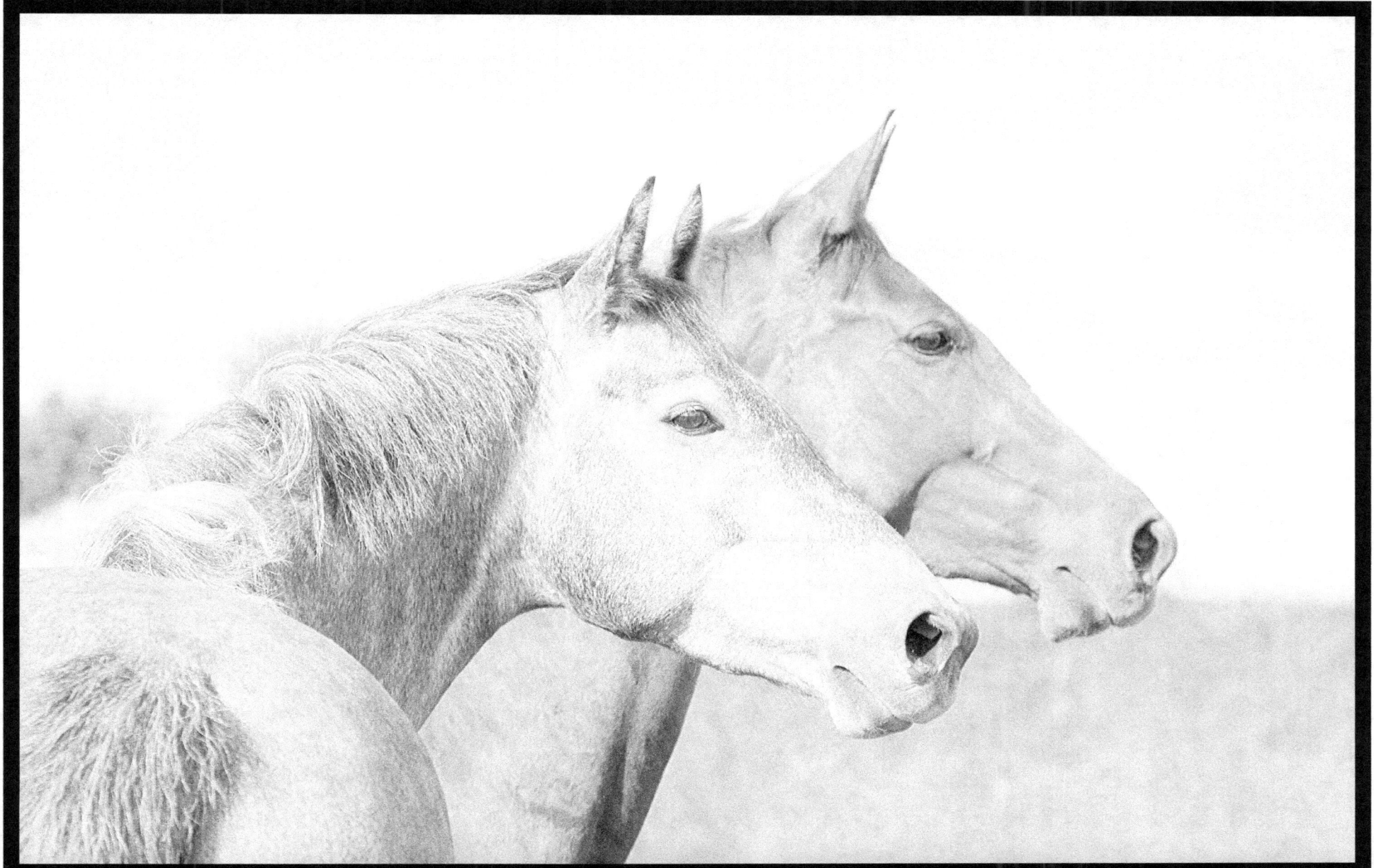

Horses Grayscale Coloring Book

Copyright © 2020 by Planet Earth

All rights reserved.
No part of this book may be reproduced without written permission of the copyright owner, except for the use of limited quotations for the purpose of book reviews.

www.ingramcontent.com/pod-product-compliance
Lightning Source LLC
Chambersburg PA
CBHW080909220526

45466CB00011BA/3522